Principles of
STAGE COMBAT
Handbook

Plate 1. "The Battle" from the William-Alan Landes/Players U.S.A. WONDRAWHOPPER, *Indian Tales.* Lance fighting (foreground, left to right) are Grey Cloud (Don Agey) and Lone Wolf (Mike Konopa). Tamahawk and shield fighting (background, left to right) are Lone Eagle (Carlos Hernandez) and Sharp Knife (Tom Cicero).

Principles of
STAGE COMBAT
Handbook

by Claude D. Kezer

PLAYERS PRESS, Inc.
P.O. Box 1132
Studio City, CA 91614-0132

PRINCIPLES OF STAGE COMBAT HANDBOOK

© Copyright, 1995, by Claude D. Kezer, and PLAYERS PRESS, Inc.
ISBN 0-88734-650-2
Library of Congress Catalog Number: 94-43588

Printed in the U.S.A.

Simultaneously published
U.S.A., Canada, U.K., and Australia

Library of Congress Cataloging-in-Publications Data

Kezer, Claude D.
       Principles of stage combat / by Claude D. Kezer. --2nd ed.
           p.   cm.
       Includes index.
       ISBN 0-88734-650-2
       1. Stage fighting.   I. Title.
PN2071.F5K49 1994
792' . 028--dc20

                                               94-43588
                                               CIP

PREFACE

Theatre is fraught with hazards, many of which are not in the control of the actor. However, those hazards which are within the control of the actor should not go unchecked.

Each year performers on the stage are hurt, and not too infrequently killed, because they and their directors lacked the necessary knowledge for safely creating excitement and realism in dramatic scenes which contain violence.

We have enough problems with actors simply falling off the stage, down stairs, and against furniture. We should not compound our problems by asking actors to engage in stage combat if we don't understand the disciplines required to insure the greatest possible degree of safety.

Surely the student who prankishly put the live round of ammunition in a pistol didn't want someone actually to be shot onstage; the director who should have known that a 1 x 12 piece of white pine will split on contact with a knife thrust didn't want to see an actor stabbed to death; the director who failed to check the flexibility of foils before one of them broke didn't want to see an actor run through the heart in a sword fight.

These are some of the reasons I believe a book of this nature is a must in the hands of every college and high school director of theatre—and why courses in colleges and universities covering the skills of stage-combat safety are a necessity for actors and future teacher-directors of theatre. I wrote it because I care a great deal about *my kids,* as I am sure you care about yours. Let's have excellent, exciting theatre with the greatest possible safety measures we can contrive.

Break a leg, but do it safely.

C. D. K.

ACKNOWLEDGEMENTS

From stumbling adolescence to lessons in adagio dance, from school athletics to professional theatre, from daring youth to cautious adult, my various aspects of stage-combat safety have evolved. My thanks to all who have contributed to my education.

My thanks to Christopher Gould for his expertise in editing what I had written to prepare it for submission to the publisher; to Moushegh Tourian and LaDonna Porter for their photography; to John Malone for his assistance in developing and printing the pictures; to students and friends who volunteered their time to three photo sessions; and to my department chairman, Dr. Jerry Nye, who honored my request to offer and develop such an important course which later led to the writing of this book.

My gratefulness to all those who played a part in the production of this book may be overshadowed only by the fulfillment I will feel if the benefits of this study save some person from serious harm in what is otherwise a most pleasurable vocation.

My wish for all is happiness and good health in THEATRE.

C. D. K.

Plate 2. Little John (Brodie Greer) and Will Scarlet (Tim Askew) Cudgel practicing, from William-Alan Landes'
WONDRAWHOPPER, *Robin Hood,* a Players U.S.A. production.

CONTENTS

LIST OF PHOTOGRAPHS
and ILLUSTRATIONS

Plate 3. *Bloody Jack* — Northern Michigan University, Marquette, Michigan.

INTRODUCTION

Theatre is a compact reflection of life. It is a powerful influence on the public.

Whether we see the show live, on TV, or at the movies; in a nightclub, on the street corner, or on the sports-field, we are moved by those elements which are the vital aspects of theatre. Plot, character, thought, and language are what cause the observer to laugh or cry, be tranquil or furious, frustrated or patient, even frightened or fear-less. With these elements, we can teach, lead, push, or shape our audiences in whatever direction we wish them to go.

Theatre is the only art form that engages all of the other fine arts in one discipline. We use pictorial or graphic art as well as make-up; sound and music; architecture; clothing design; lighting design and movies; dance movement; creative writing—not to mention acting.

Theatre can bring into focus the totality of aesthetic appreciation. When it carries out this task effectively, all aspects of the production point toward the theme and seldom call attention to themselves. This is the ideal effect we wish to create for the audience. However, as teachers in educational theatre, our jobs do not start or stop with entertaining the audience. Our primary job is to enable our students to understand, recognize, and apply in all their intricacies the elements of theatre mentioned above.

To explain fully this primary job, one would have to launch into a dissertation which would require volumes. Briefly, however, the job of the teacher of theatre is to help the student *cope* with every demand made of him or her in all the practical elements of production. If this entailed only a mastery of the technical aspects of theatre, the task would be difficult enough; but we must add to that task the job of directing the actors in portraying their roles. Here they must not only learn to *cope* with someone else's problems realistically, but also be willing to *risk* baring emotions publicly. At the same time they must exercise the craft of theatre: how to move; what voice to use, what tonality, what gesture; how to play lights, costumes, sound, stage position, body position, set, properties, and so forth.

The public needs entertainment. We have a responsibility to fill that need. We work for professionalism; we expect our students to have professional attitudes; we develop professional actors, and professional teachers to further encourage talented and gifted young people to satisfy their needs for creativity and the public need for quality entertainment.

As we look at the various aspects of theatre for which we develop programs and in which we teach our students to excel, there is one area that has been markedly overlooked: **stage combat and safety**.

All too frequently students are killed or badly injured on stage as they attempt to make the scene "realistic." Most of these accidents happen because many directors do not know how to direct physical conflict on stage, and to do it safely.

Go to any magician and ask what magic is. Of course you know the answer—magic is illusion. We talk of the "magic of theatre"—and that magic also is illusion.

1

Plate 4. *Macbeth* — Southwestern Oklahoma State University.

2

Chapter 1
DEVELOPING FLEXIBILITY, STRENGTH, and QUICK RESPONSE

The realistic stunt in stage combat is about 50 percent illusion, 45 percent acting, 3 percent reality, and 2 percent bump. To be able to carry off the illusion, the actor must be in good physical condition. He or she should begin each day's class with 15 minutes of exercise. Some of the following procedures should help to develop flexibility, strength, and quick reflexes.

Exercises

1. For physical conditioning:

Deep knee bends—10

Feet wide apart—touch hands flat on the floor—15

　　touch outside of left heel with right hand; rotate (right heel/left hand)—15

　　touch floor behind and between legs to greatest reach—15

Feet together—touch hands flat on the floor—10

　　twist right to left, arms parallel to floor, at waist; rotate—15

Feet apart—bend at waist and rotate body to side, back, side, front; reverse—15

Jumping jacks—15

Feet in ballet position—right foot: 1, 2, 3, 4, 5; left foot: same

Prep and leap—make half knee bend and leap in air, working for soft landing (i.e., toes and knees absorbing shock); leap straight up, forward, backward, and to each side 3 times each, for total of 15 leaps

On back—lift knees, leaving feet on floor; arch back and support weight on feet and head

　　lift feet 6 inches; hold till it hurts, patting stomach to relieve tension

On stomach—do 10-15 push-ups

　　arch back and rock like a rocking horse

With partner (sitting)—face each other (legs spread apart with feet touching); reach across and grasp hands; rotate, pulling each other as far forward as waist will allow—10

　　do 15 sit-ups, with partner holding down feet

2. For quick response and awareness:

With partner—play patty-cake as fast as possible

　　A holds hands 8 inches apart; B attempts to pass hand quickly between; A tries to catch B's hand; rotate

　　(both with hands at side, facing each other) A starts to slap at B; B responds by blocking slap with open hand

Follow leader—leader (in front of class) does patterns of hands and feet movement (e.g., slap rhythm on hands or legs or body); group follows

With partner—A and B touch palms (A palms up, B palms down); as each looks in the other's eyes (not at hands), A quickly moves one hand and tries to slap the top of one of B's hands; B tries to avoid being hit; rotate

Other than being in good physical condition in order to be able to withstand the rigors of stage combat, one of the first responsibilities the actor has to develop is total awareness of environment. The actor participating in stage combat must be totally aware of his or her surroundings: set, costumes, properties, the lip of the stage, the other actors, and so forth.

Exercises

1. Set up obstacles on the stage. Have actors walk through the entire course with their eyes closed (blinking in reverse), opening their eyes on the director's count every five seconds. This procedure should help the actors learn to take in all surroundings quickly and to know their places in relation to those of the other actors. It should

help develop judgment of distances, peripheral vision, and alertness.

2. Have the actors lie down on the stage in close proximity to one another with legs and arms extended wide and at odd angles. Have each actor take his turn walking through the mass of bodies without stepping on anyone. This exercise must begin slowly and increase in speed until each actor passing through the maze is moving at a running, jumping pace. (The actors on the floor during this exercise must lie very still.)

3. Have the actors walk the front edge of the stage as though it were a tightrope. This should help them develop balance. (A 2 x 4 nailed on its edge on the stage also is good for this exercise.)

The concept of total awareness should be stressed continually. During sessions you may wish to alter exercises. Following is a list of alternate procedures, to which you may wish to add some of your own.

Further Exercises

1. Have three actors stand with arms extended parallel to the floor, hands open. Have them twist from the waist so that the hands, together, scribe a circle. Have other actors walk between the flailing arms, ducking and dodging.

2. Have the actors form a human maze of arches, barricades, or webs through which a traveler must pass. The traveler is permitted one good look at the setup and then must proceed through it with eyes closed.

3. One student (the observer) sitting in a front seat in the classroom has his vision masked by the instructor. Other students, one or two at a time, execute an action which the observer is allowed to see no more than one second. The observer must then reconstruct verbally the details of the action. This helps to develop memory, but, more significantly, it is highly effective in contributing to instantaneous observation and awareness. Rotate members of the class in the positions of observer and performers.

Presumably, actors have begun by now to think about awareness and safety. Nevertheless, daily routines should be continued and should proceed slowly. Actors frequently get over-anxious and want to go at full speed. Always guard against this. All good stunts potentially are dangerous and always should be approached with a yellow light until the timing and concentration have been perfected.

Equally important is the fact that the body must be in good shape to participate in safe stage combat. Do not shirk this responsibility to your actors. Each session should begin with at least ten to fifteen minutes of exercises.

Plate 5. *Gammer Gurton's Needle* — Backstage, Inc., Schulenburg, Texas.

4

NOTES

NOTES

Chapter 2
LEARNING TO BREAK FALLS

Practically all scenes involving stage combat conclude with one or more actors taking falls; or falls may be laced throughout an entire scene. Learning to fall properly guarantees safety for the actor as well as excitement for the audience. Further, learning to fall properly carries another benefit: avoiding serious injury in real-life accidents.

One of our actors who had taken a course in stage combat was later cast in the lead role in *The Elephant Man.* A hood covering his head, his vision was impaired severely; and the scene was lit dimly. Because of one misstep, the elephant man took an unrehearsed tumble to the auditorium floor. Though it was only a four-foot drop, the fall potentially was quite dangerous. But thanks to relaxation, absorption or cushioning, and roll, the actor avoided injury, climbed (in character) back up onto the stage, and finished the show.

Many men are not afraid of falls. As boys, they have played games that involve puposeful or accidental falls. Women, on the other hand, sometimes are a different story. As girls, they may have been encouraged to avoid the roughhouse antics of boys and therefore, as adults,

sometimes are reluctant to take falls. Despite any such differences, however, it is important for all students to start at the beginning and progress slowly to full speed. This gives both men and women a chance to learn not to fear falling, to dispel any fright of the bump.

Exercise

Starting from a sitting position, legs extended in front, fall back to one side, extending the arm (same side) above the head (Photo 1), and slapping the floor with the flat of the hand and the forearm to break the impact on the body. Repeat this exercise several times on each side. Once this exercise can be performed comfortably, progress to a squatting position. Roll backward for this short-distance fall, performing the same technique as above. Ideally, all falls should be practiced and executed on wooden floors.

Once everyone is secure in the preceding exercise, move on to a standing, flexed-knees position. From such a position, the fall takes on a slightly different perspective and therefore entails another technique. The faller now

Photo 1

must learn to absorb the impact initially with the side of the leg. As the fall begins, (s)he must step back to the side on which the fall is to occur. If the fall is to be to the left, the left foot is placed approximately 12 inches behind the right foot with the weight on the outside of the left foot. The weight is then absorbed through curling down on the outside of the left ankle and the outside of the calf (Photo 2), knee, and thigh before landing on the left hand and forearm (Photo 3). The head should land on the shoulder and biceps (Photo 4). This technique must be practiced many times, on both left and right sides.

Photo 2

Photo 3

Photo 4

8

The forward fall is done essentially the same way. In a fall to the right, the weight is placed on the outside of the right foot. The actor curls down on the outside of the ankle (Photos 5 and 6), calf, knee, thigh, and the right side of the body, with the right hand extended above the head. Open hand and forearm break the fall. The head should land on the shoulder and biceps.

Of course once the fall is broken, the actor should continue to act according to what is required in the scene: e.g., roll to an unconscious relaxed or crumpled position or regain footing for continuance of the fight. It is important to make the fall look real (Photo 3) and at the same time to make it with the utmost safety for the actor.

Photo 5

Photo 6

NOTES

NOTES

Photo 7

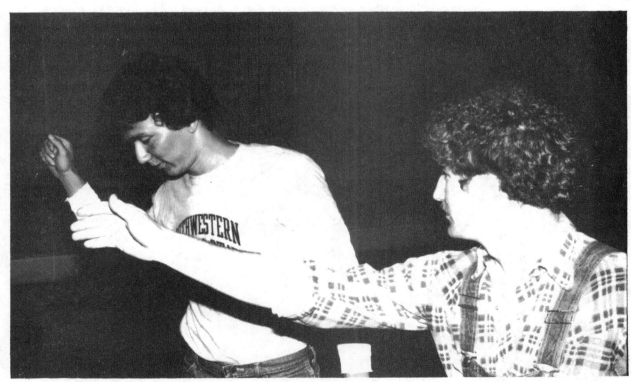

Photo 8a

12

Chapter 3
SLAPPING and HITTING

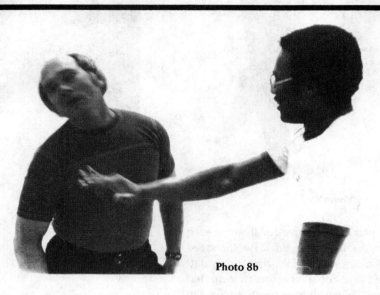

Photo 8b

As we proceed to more physical kinds of combat, it is important to remember that on the legit stage we cannot be as elaborate as in the movies. In the movies or television, film can be stopped, make-up added, and cutting and splicing techniques used—options unavailable in theatre. While we must rely on illusion or sleight of hand, the celluloid media, because of the time and distance between production and viewing, may use more graphic portrayals.

Slap my Face

A student chosen to do this exercise will feel uncomfortable about striking a teacher, but students need to be shown that a slap really doesn't hurt very much when it is done properly. First, any rings need to be removed from the slapping hand. Hand and fingers should be slightly cupped and make contact with the tips of the fingers at the turn of the jawbone and the palm at the chin (Photo 7). It is important to measure the distance of the reach, making sure that the distance is the same each time that the slap is practiced or done in a performance. If the distance and timing are not right, the slap can end up on the neck or ear, or even miss the target altogether. Pre-

paring one good slap to deliver before an audience demands many in practice. The actor must slap quickly and spontaneously to draw credibility and empathy from an audience.

The slap does not stop on the cheek but continues the follow-through, which gives it credibility (Photo 8). The actor receiving the slap must not betray the fact that the slap is coming, for that would ruin the entire effect. He or she must receive the slap as a complete surprise, and the reaction should suit the force of the blow. A light slap will turn the head only slightly; in the case of a somewhat harder slap, the head and body should turn. A forceful slap should knock the actor down. To paraphrase Shakespeare, I advise: Suit the reaction to the action and o'erstep not the modesty of nature.

The timing of a slap must be correct. (Remember the importance of *total awareness!*) Even though he or she must convince the audience that the slap is totally unexpected, the actor not only must be prepared for the imminent blow, but also must time his reaction so that just as the hand meets the face he turns his head accordingly in order to reduce the force of the impact—just as a boxer "slips" punches. (Going with the blow reduces the forcefulness of the real contact.)

Have actors practice this fistic attack with sound effects and reactions numerous times, moving at half speed. When they have become fairly secure, have the actors pair off and "knock" each other down, again taking falls as previously learned.

Photo 9

Photo 10

Have all students pair off and practice slapping each other. Going slow at the beginning, increase the speed and force gradually. Cheeks will redden—that is only natural—but this is a good time for good actors to learn that there's a price to be paid. When all have practiced the slap and feel relatively comfortable with it, have two at a time demonstrate at least three different degrees of force, the last one strong enough to knock the receiver down. (The receiver should employ the backfall learned in preceding exercises.) Try to get both actors to perform a convincing show. Since verbal battles typically accompany physical attacks and verbal responses accompany physical reactions, teach the actors to grunt and groan.

Hitting with Fists

The actors having learned the slap, it is only natural that fistics should follow. Striking another actor with a fist can look either super or ridiculous on stage, depending on how well it is done. The blow must be telegraphed (hinted at or presaged) for the sake of safety; it must carry the appropriate sound effect for the sake of realism. Again, timing, distance, and total awareness are musts. A blow to the face has to miss the receiver by at least an inch or two. As the fist goes past his face, the actor must act as though catching the full force of the punch (Photo 9). At the instant that the blow would land, the striker slaps his own chest, stomach, or leg with the open opposite (upstage) hand, thus creating a sound similar to an actual blow.

Photo 11

14

The next fistic attack is a body blow. Unlike the face attack, this is not a punch that can be carried through. The body punch must stop in the body, pulled just as contact is made (Photo 10). The actor receiving the blow reacts by folding over the stomach punch (Photo 10) or by falling away from the kidney punch (Photo 11). This kind of pulled punch must be practiced a great deal before it can be delivered with authority and credibility.

Have the actors begin with slow motion, gradually increasing their pace. Remember that the punch must be made with force yet pulled back just at the point of contact. If you have an actor who finds it difficult to stop his punch, have him practice throwing punches at a wall, chair, or other solid object. Out of fear of hurting himself, this actor will learn to pull his punch at just the right instant.

Elbows are good weapons against an attacker who has both arms around the body. The elbow is driven back into the body of the attacker, pulled—like all other types of fistics and kicks—at the point of contact. If both arms are pinned in the grasp of the attacker, the hand can be directed to the crotch, or a foot stomp can be used to break the hold.

In still another kind of fistic blow, two hands, fingers clasped, swing like a club; this kind of blow is especially effective in creating a feeling of great weight and strength behind an attack. Remember that the fists are not to come in contact with the victim. The fists are pulled if the blow is to the stomach; they must miss by a short distance if aimed at the face. Again, the degree of reaction should match the force of the attack, which is great in this instance. If this kind of blow is aimed at the back of the victim, the punch is pulled although the forearms actually do make contact with the back (Photo 12), pushing the victim to a fall.

Photo 12

Putting it Together

Improvise an interlude of combat which employs all of the learned contact and falls to this point. For example, place two people standing on stage talking. An argument ensues. One actor slaps the other semi-hard; the other slaps the first harder, knocking him down. The first actor rises, strikes the other in the stomach, straightens up proud of his accomplishment, only to be knocked down by the other with a fist to the face. You may devise any such routine, having all actors carry it out. Those who are not participating at the moment should watch from the front, getting the full effect; encourage response and comment concerning the effectiveness of each demonstration. (You may have to remind the performers to be vocal and to "act" like they're being hurt during the routine.)

Plate 6. *The Little Match Girl* — Schulenburg, Texas, Junior High School.

15

NOTES

Chapter 4
TUMBLES

Photo 13b

Shoulder Tumble

How many people cannot recall ever turning somersaults? Yet we've all done it; it's fun. Even some species of animals have been observed enjoying somersaults. But even though we've all done somersaults before, there still is a right way as well as a wrong way to do it. Doing it right, no one gets hurt; doing it wrong, an actor can injure his/her neck, head, or back. Since safety should be the overriding concern, let's learn to do somersaults right.

Begin with the forward shoulder tumble. The students should learn to tumble on both sides, but it's best to have them begin on the side of their handedness. Start from a squatting position, putting both hands on the floor with the heels of the hands about 18 inches from the toes of the shoes. As the legs straighten with a little push which gives momentum to the tumble, tuck the chin down toward the chest and cock the head to that shoulder which is *not* making contact with the floor—for example, to the left shoulder when tumbling on the right side (Photo 13a). The hands should support the weight of the body to insure that the head clears the floor, and the weight of the tumble should be caught on the back of that shoulder on whose side the tumble is made. Have all students practice the tumble many times, alternating sides.

Forward Tumble

After they have mastered the shoulder tumble, students should proceed to the forward tumble. This one is done in the same way as the shoulder tumble, except that the head does not cock to one side. The chin tucks deep into the chest while the hands and arms support the weight in order for the head to clear the floor. The weight of the tumble is caught on the upper back (Photo 13b). Have students practice this tumble several times.

After the shoulder tumble and the forward tumble have been learned from a squatting position, have the actors perform them from a half-crouching position and then from a standing position.

Once each of these tumbles has been thoroughly mastered, you can add some flair by entering them through an aerial approach. Usually only the more athletic actors will want to try this. It is accomplished through leaping-diving through the air in the manner of an awkward front-header, landing on the hands to break the initial fall, and then continuing on through the shoulder tumble.

Know your Space

It is important for the actor to know his or her own body, its capabilities, and its limitations—completely. He or she should know the distance of a normal stride, as well as the amount of space on stage required for a fall. Place a line of tape three feet long on the floor, center stage, and follow each of these procedures:

1. From a point further than normal stepping distance from the line, have the actors take a long stride to place the toe of their reaching foot just behind the line.

2. Repeat the same exercise, but now have the heel land just beyond the line.

3. At three paces from the line, have the actors leap in order to accomplish the same results.

4. Have each actor lie down, in turn, with his or her heels on the line, measuring the distance from the line to the shoulders. Then have the actors do a shoulder tumble or a forward tumble with the aim of landing their heels on the line. Don't put any marking at the point where the shoulders are to make contact with the stage floor. The actor must instinctively know this distance and be able to estimate it at any time.

Backward Tumble

The backward tumble is best started from a squatting position. The buttocks absorb the initial part of the fall, and the tumble proceeds as the actor rolls over a curved back and shoulder (either shoulder) with the head turned to the side opposite the shoulder that is supporting the tumble. Next, have the actor move to a half-standing position, using the technique that was learned earlier for the backward fall; he should then step into the fall and take the tumble. Finally, from a standing position, the actor steps back into the fall and takes the tumble. Students should practice this tumble going over both shoulders.

Putting it Together

When the actors have gained mastery of the tumbles, set up short scenes of fistic encounter which employ the tumbles in falls or knockdowns. Again, have all the actors do the same routines, establishing a specific spot on the floor where you want the actors' feet to land on the tumble.

Plate 7. *Don't Print That!* — Theatre Southwest, Houston.

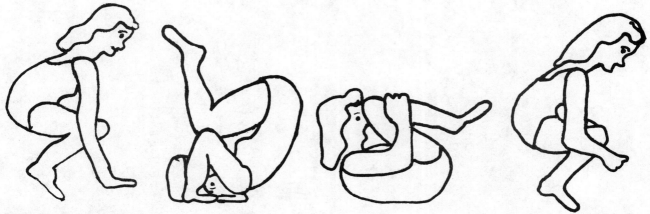

Basic Front or Forward Roll

Basic Back Roll.

Plate 8. Tumbling.

19

NOTES

Chapter 5
ROLLING and FALLING DOWN STAIRS

In back of the author's house is a very steep hill. In the lush green grass or in deep snow, children love to roll laterally down that hill. This is, again, an activity that many of us have done in our youth.

The lateral roll is another important activity in stage combat safety. It is fun for the audience to watch; and, more importantly, it is the only safe way to roll down a flight of stairs. Have actors practice the roll several times on the stage before they attempt it on stairs. After the practice on stage, proceed to a wooden flight of stairs and have the actors roll down them in a carefully controlled, slow-motion fall. Continue increasing the speed until the actors feel secure in this fall. Now we can move on to falls down stairs.

Falling Down Stairs

Falling down stairs is dangerous . . . unless it is done properly. We will present two approaches. First is the fall caused by a knockdown or push. If a push causes a fall, it is best for that push to be executed at the top of the stairs, far enough back to allow the actor to fall on a flat surface (landing) prior to the roll down the stairs (Photos 14 and 15). This roll must be carefully controlled. It must be lateral so it is a roll, not a tumble (forward or backward). A highly controlled tumble can be worked into the fall if the stairs are long enough, but then the control must go back to a roll. Another good technique for creating audience tension is to control the roll to a "hurt" standing recovery two steps from the bottom and to do a forward fall from the last two steps. The important thing to remember is that the fall down stairs must be highly controlled and lateral.

The second cause of a fall down stairs is a faint or a shot. In the case of a faint, the actor simply slumps up the stairs and begins the lateral roll. This fall must seem much more relaxed than the one described above. But even though it must *appear* to be very loose, it still must be under careful expert control, or the actor can be hurt. If a shot causes the fall, the actor must react in the direction of the shot. For example, a shot from below would knock the actor up the stairs; one from the side would knock him against the wall; one from above would knock him down the stairs. Each is easily handled except the last one. If the shot does come from above, the actor must be able to use a hand rail to stop his forward pitch down the stairs and set up the lateral roll.

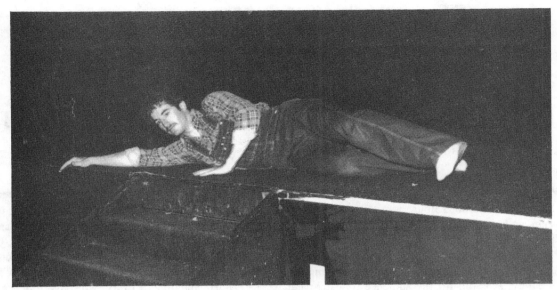

Photo 14

Photo 15

22

NOTES

Plate 9. *Twelve Dancing Princesses* — Casa Mañana Playhouse, Ft. Worth, Tex. © Norman Bradford.

Chapter 6
STOMPING and KICKING

A "fair" fight on stage would be a bore; actors must learn to fight dirty. It's time to teach them kicks and stomps. Television wrestlers are especially good at this kind of stage combat. If their antics caused the injuries they appear to, their careers would be very short. On stage, all stomps and kicks must be pulled, or else the impact of the blow must be absorbed by the person delivering it.

Kicks

Let's begin with kicks by having the attacker and the victim standing. If the kick is delivered from behind the victim to his legs, it must be delivered with the top of the foot (toes pointed) or with the side of the foot, the instep (Photo 16). If the kick is delivered to the posterior, the foot position should be the same. If it is delivered to the small of the back, it should be given with the top of the foot or the flat of the sole (Photo 17). Each of these

Photo 16

Photo 17

Photo 18a

kicks must be pulled just before the moment of contact. This requires lots of practice—practice kicks against walls or furniture which will require the actor to pull the kick to avoid hurting himself.

When actors pair off to begin practice, slow motion is essential. Timing reaction to the kick is a necessary ingredient of the stunt. Timing can be gauged from the action immediately preceding in the fight. But if the kick begins the fight, a signal has to be given to start the timing. A stage signal can be easily brought off without the audience's being at all aware of it. For example, a signal might be a sharp but slight expulsion of air, a slight click of the tongue, or a concealed, quiet snap of the fingers. The kicker and the victim must practice counting together so that their timing is entirely accurate. "Unexpected" attacks must be practiced repeatedly if they are to work safely.

Kicks to the Front

If the kick is to be administered to the shins, it must be given with the instep of the kicker; if to the crotch, with the top of the foot or knee; if to the stomach, with the top of the foot (from the side) or the knee (from the side); if to the head, with the top of the foot (from the side) or the knee (from the front or side). Again, each kick must be pulled just before the moment of contact. *Remember that the point of contact from the front will always be the victim's hands* (Photo 18). All kicks to the front of the body must be caught (blocked) by the victim's hands, covering the point of contact.

Photo 18b

Kicks to the Crotch or Head

If the kick is to be delivered to a prone victim, it should come from upstage so it can be masked from the audience's view (Photo 19). The kick can be administered to the victim's head or body. Such a blow should be administered by kicking to the desired point on the floor just prior to making contact with the victim (Photo 20). The follow-through is carried out by allowing the knee to continue past the point of contact. Executed properly, and with the proper response from the victim, this stunt can be very effective.

Photo 20

Photo 19a

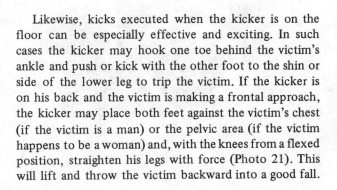

Photo 19b

Photo 21

Likewise, kicks executed when the kicker is on the floor can be especially effective and exciting. In such cases the kicker may hook one toe behind the victim's ankle and push or kick with the other foot to the shin or side of the lower leg to trip the victim. If the kicker is on his back and the victim is making a frontal approach, the kicker may place both feet against the victim's chest (if the victim is a man) or the pelvic area (if the victim happens to be a woman) and, with the knees from a flexed position, straighten his legs with force (Photo 21). This will lift and throw the victim backward into a good fall.

27

Photo 22a

On the other hand, with both kicker and victim in the previous positions, the kicker may place his feet in the approaching victim's stomach, and let the momentum of the victim carry forward (the kicker's feet hold up the victim); at this point the victim places his hands on the floor or the shoulders of the kicker, resulting in a throw into a forward roll (Photo 22). In this case the heads should be cocked to opposite sides to insure that they don't make contact with each other. Having the victim's hands on the floor or the kicker's shoulders insures that the victim's head will not make contact with the floor. The weight of the fall should be absorbed by the round of the back of the victim.

Work out a fight routine using the various types of kicks learned in this chapter. For example, Actor A makes an insulting remark to Actor B, who happens to be walking by. Actor B turns and kicks A in the posterior. Actor A turns and kicks B on the shins. Actor B knocks A down and continues to kick A while he is down. Actor A swivels on his back and kicks B in the chest (or pelvic area). Actor B charges A and A kicks B in the stomach; B rolls over A (Photo 22c) and lies on the floor "knocked out."

Photo 22b

Photo 22c

Stomps

Kicker and victim should begin this stunt standing. If the stomp is to be delivered to the victim's feet, the action must be carried out quickly and accurately. It takes a moment for the audience to shift their eyes from the actors' faces to the floor; so this stunt is relatively easy to carry off convincingly. As the foot comes down for the stomp, the toes should be raised, and the heel should make contact with the floor loudly while the kicker's toes (raised) stop just over the victim's foot. The reaction of the victim completes the stunt.

If the victim is on the floor, the stomping of hands, arms, legs, or whatever is carried out in the same manner (Photo 23) as the foot stomp, described above. A note of caution: if any stomp or blow is directed toward the neck, it must be to the side or back and must be pulled or masked, or caught by the victim's hands.

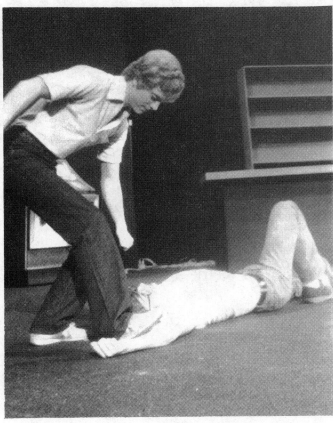

Photo 23a

Photo 23b

Photo 24

A third form of stomp is executed by jumping into the air and landing on the victim with the knees apparently striking a vital area. (If you've ever watched television wrestling, you've probably seen this stunt many times.) The weight of the impact is caught by the foot of the stomper; the knee is stopped or pulled just before the moment of contact (Photos 24 and 25). As with the other routines, these stunts call for a great deal of practice and control, beginning in slow motion.

Knee Lifts and Putting it all Together

There is one more use of the knee that is effective in stage combat—the knee lift. This maneuver usually will follow a foot stomp or a fistic encounter to the stomach—something that causes the victim to bend forward at the waist. With the victim in this bent-over position, the attacker covers the upper part of the victim's body and hits him in the head or upper chest with his knee. The victim's hands catch this blow, the force of the knee lift causing a reaction that carries the victim up into the air and backward for a fall, tumble, or roll.

Do several routines using these skills. Let students improvise fights using kicks and stomps.

Photo 25

NOTES

NOTES

Chapter 7
FALLING FROM HEIGHT

At the movies we have all seen stunt men and women fall from buildings and out of planes, helicopters, and trees. These movie stunt people have all kinds of sophisticated equipment to assist them and to insure their safety.

In the legitimate theatre, however, it is difficult to imagine an actor's ever falling more than eight or ten feet. The author once had to take a fall in a war scene at the Dallas State Fair Musicals production of *The Vagabond King*. It was a blind fall—one that involved dropping backward off a battlement with two catchers positioned to break the fall. The point is that even a relatively short fall such as this requires catchers or heavy padding on which to land. If a fall from these short heights is to be brought off in sight of the audience, it must be done under extreme control.

Forward and Backward Falls

In teaching actors how to fall from heights, a four-foot-high platform is a good place to start. Begin by having students simply jump from the platform. Show them how to cushion their falls by flexing their knees upon impact. Next have them leave the platform by leaping into the air. Most actors will increase the distance of their falls by one or two feet, and you now can inform them that they are falling five or six feet.

When all the actors have become fairly comfortable with jumping off the four-foot platform and landing on their feet, it is time to have them engage in a fall to the floor upon impact. Here the knees absorb the initial shock and the controlled fall absorbs the rest. Next, have your actors jump off the platform backward. Go through the same routine—leap and fall on impact. This backward jump from height should be marked or spotted. That is, there should be on the landing at least one person on each side of the falling actor. These people need to be there to make sure that the falling actor does not accidentally lose control and get hurt.

Side Falls

Next, the actors should learn to roll off the sides of the platform. As they roll, they should position them-

Photo 26

selves so that their feet go over the side first. In this way, the feet hit the floor, cushioning the fall; the rest of the fall should proceed as explained above.

The second kind of rolling fall from height is a highly controlled one. It must be done correctly because the actor who is falling must go off the stage or platform face down, laterally. This means that the falling actor must be on his side just at the edge of the platform so that after his roll he is face down in space. This kind of fall is broken with the hands, forearms, and feet (Photo 27, p. 24).

The third kind of rolling fall takes the actor off the platform head first. In this fall, the hands make contact with the floor first; then the legs help to break the fall further; and finally there is a roll to break the shock (Photo 26).

These kinds of falls can be done from heights up to eight or ten feet onto a bare stage floor; however, it is not wise for anyone who is not unusually athletic and agile to attempt a fall of more than five feet.

Do routines employing these skills.

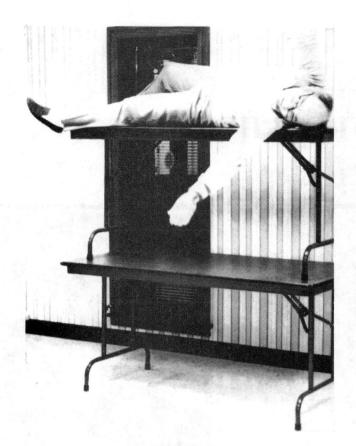

Photo 27a

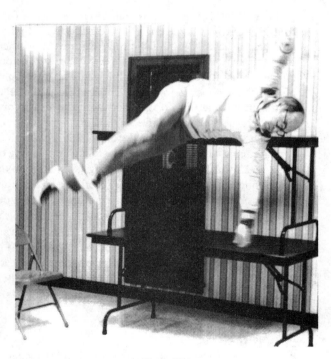

Photo 27c

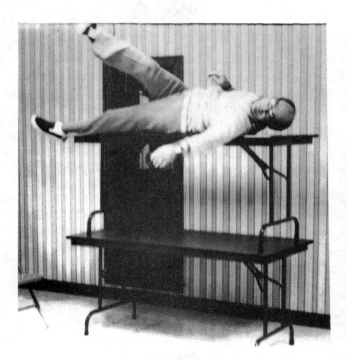

Photo 27b

Photo 27d

34

NOTES

NOTES

Chapter 8
THROWS

There are many ways to "throw" a person, from simple pushes to more complex procedures. The most important thing to remember in carrying out throws is that the actor who is being thrown is always the one in control of the stunt; he or she needs only a little help from the thrower. As in previous chapters, let's begin with the simpler procedures and then move to some of the more complex ones.

Simple Throws

Two actors stand face to face, the thrower placing his hands on the waist of the other actor (the receptor). The receptor puts his hands on the forearms or shoulders of the thrower (Photo 28). Each prepares for the throw by bending knees to provide lift. The thrower lifts and pushes the receptor backward; at the same time, the receptor leaps and pushes off the forearms or shoulders of the thrower, helping to lift and propel himself (Photo 29). The receptor then lands on his feet and enters a back fall or a backward tumble. This throw may be directed to the right or left by the receptor's jumping in the desired direction.

The Run Around

The next throw requires lots of space. The thrower does nothing but hold on to the hand of the receptor. The receptor runs around the thrower (who serves as a pivot or anchor) while acting as though he is being flung with force around the circle. At the proper moment of release, the receptor simply lets go of the thrower's hand

Photo 28

Photo 29

Photo 30

and propels himself into a series of spinning lateral rolls, a forward tumble, or a backward tumble. Remember that the receptor must be in complete control of this throw.

The Arm Throw

If a throw is to be preceded by an overhand knife attack* or a fistic roundhouse punch, the thrower intercepts the attacking arm by grasping its wrist with his hand (thumb down) on the side from which the attack is coming (if, for example, the attack comes from a right hand, the thrower makes his grasp with his left hand). Once the attacker's wrist has been secured, the thrower reaches across and secures another hand hold on the attacker's arm just above the elbow, second hand thumb up (Photo 30). Now the thrower steps in front of the attacker with his right foot to secure a position where the thrower's right shoulder is placed in the armpit of the attacker. At this moment the attacker's arm is drawn down; the thrower's back is bent into the lift; and the attacker is thrown across the right side of the thrower (Photo 31). This procedure can end with a lateral roll or backward tumble.

Photo 31

*Note: An important aspect of the knife attack is that the attacker never expects to complete the attack. He should stop or check his thrust at the point where contact is expected to be made.

If a knife is involved in this stunt, there are two things that can be done to insure safety. The attacker may be disarmed by the thrower's shaking the knife free and "clearing" it (casting it aside away from the throw area), or the knife may be held in the attacker's hand throughout the throw with control maintained by the thrower's holding securely onto the wrist of the attacker. Disarming the attacker may then occur after he has landed on the floor.

The Hip Throw

In this maneuver it is especially important that the attacker (the receptor) be carefully positioned. He should begin by having one arm raised as he attacks. (Assuming that this throw comes from the right side, let's have him raise his right arm.) The thrower should move to his position (right side to right side, facing in opposite directions). The thrower grabs the right wrist of the receptor with his left hand, reaches across the receptor's chest, securing his right hand in the armpit of the receptor. The thrower steps with his right foot behind the receptor and pulls forward with his right arm while extending his right hip (Photo 32). The receptor will then take a back fall with his head toward the thrower (Photo 33). The thrower holds on to the receptor's right wrist throughout this throw for safety.

Photo 32

Photo 33

The Aerial Flip

This throw is dangerous and cannot be practiced in slow motion. It must be done with a strong thrower and an athletic receptor. This is a complete forward flip with the receptor's feet, body, and hands off the floor. Let's set this throw up for a right-handed receptor who plays an attacker. The attacker starts by swinging or punching at the thrower. The thrower controls the attacker's right hand with his own left hand, thumb down. The thrower's right hand then joins the left hand with a reverse grip, thumb up (Photo 34), while the thrower steps under the attacker's right arm, still maintaining the two-handed grip, to a position to the right of and slightly behind the attacker (Photo 35). The thrower then with a pendulum swing lifts the attacker's right wrist high (approximately to the height of his own shoulder), and the attacker leaps into the air into a forward roll (Photos 36 and 37). The attacker should land with his feet breaking the fall (Photo 38) and then go into a fall or forward shoulder roll. Again, this stunt is only for the most athletic actors; definitely not all should be encouraged to try. If a knife is involved in the attack, the thrower's grip must be maintained; otherwise, the thrower may release the attacker's wrist at the conclusion of the throw.

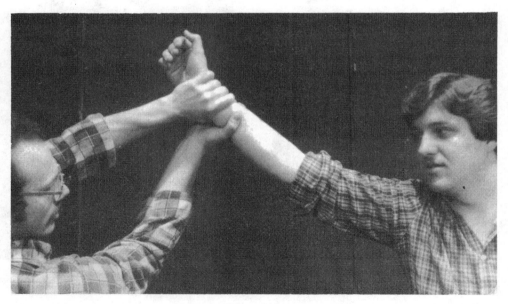

Photo 34

Photo 35

Photo 36

Photo 37

Photo 38

The Hair Throw

Hair can be used effectively in a throw. If both hands are used, the thrower can have his hands full yet still control the receptor by actually holding the head between his hands. If only one hand is used, the thrower grabs the hair while the receptor grasps the thrower's wrist with both hands; therefore, the weight of the throw is supported by the arms of the receptor (Photo 39). This kind of throw usually ends with a lateral roll.

The Head Throw

If an attack comes from behind and the grasp is around the waist or chest yet not pinning the arms, the thrower can reach back over one shoulder with both hands, clasp hands behind the head of the attacker, thrust the hip on the side of the over-the-shoulder reach, and bend forward. This throw will put the receptor over the hip into a forward landing in front of the attacker. Incidentally, the attacker must release his grasp at the point of the throw.

Photo 39a

Photo 39b

NOTES

NOTES

Chapter 9
CHOKING

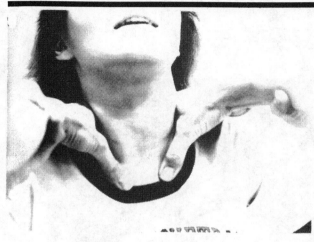

Photo 40a

some of the weight and control the action, and the attacker can support some of the weight with his or her fingers at the back of the neck.

When the strangling is masked (either by the attacker's body or by some article of furniture), the fingers are placed around the base of the neck and the thumbs are on the collar bones (Photo 40). In this case, the victim again holds on to the attacker's wrists or arms for support, finally releasing to "limp arms and hands," signifying death or unconsciousness.

Most actors consider their voices a basic, if not the most important, tool of their trade. Consequently, they can be very touchy about anyone's laying hands on their throats.

The larynx is a fragile cartilage that may get infected, bruised, or even crushed. Whenever damage is inflicted upon the larynx, it affects the production of the voice, from minor irritation to total loss. Real choking involves sustained pressure on or damage to the larynx. Choking in stage combat, on the other hand, avoids actual contact or pressure to the larynx or to any part of the front of the throat.

Choking a person on stage can be another thriller for the audience, but it must be carefully carried out by skillful actors. If the audience is to view the choking, with the attack coming from the front, the hands of the choker must be clearly in sight and must cover the neck of the victim with thumbs overlapping in front of the throat and above the larynx. In this way, the tension from the hands can be applied to the side of the neck, in order to create the illusion of pressure on the throat. The victim can hold the wrists or arms of the choker and support

Photo 40b

A strangling attack which comes from behind should find the attacker's hands covering the neck, with pressure exerted only on the sides, and the thumbs at the back of the neck to set up the muscular tension in the arms (Photo 41). Practice strangulation with the aim of creating the greatest appearance of tension with the most comfort for the victim.

If the choking is to be done with an arm around the neck, the tension should be set up in the arm and body of the attacker with no real pressure on the neck of the victim. Remember that a choking scene is a moment of high tension for the audience. It must show tension in the attacker's musculature without placing real pressure or stricture on any part of the front of the victim's neck.

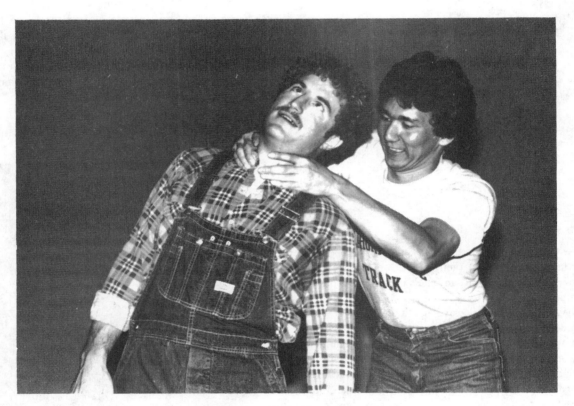

Photo 41

NOTES

NOTES

Chapter 10
USING KNIVES

Photo 42

Plate 10. *Desert Men* — Ohio State University.

Actors often become blasé about the props they use over and over in rehearsals and must constantly be reminded that knives are dangerous. A knife with a blade that does not lock never should be used on stage; blades must be either fixed or automatic locking. Cutting edges must be blunted to the point that they will not cut. The point of the knife, on the other hand, must remain sharp if the effectiveness of the stunt is to be maintained. Since even a dull blade with a dull point can injure or kill, *extreme* caution must be exercised continually. *Total awareness is an absolute must.*

If the tip of the blade is to be held against the victim, the attacker's grasp on the knife must be such that if for any reason the victim should press against the tip, the knife will slide away from him or her through the attacker's hand. The attacker must show tension in his hand and arm while at the same time having only a loose hold on the knife.

A "stabbing" must be masked from the audience in all cases. This allows the audience to imagine the worst, while providing for the safety of the actors. Whenever a stabbing is to take place on stage, the knife comes in point first—*prior to contact*. The mask is effected at this point. Behind the mask, the hand is turned so that the knife lies flat against the victim's body (fingers against the body in an overhand attack and away from the body in an underhand attack). This technique is followed whether the attack comes from the front or back.

If during the fight the combatants are locked in each other's grasp, *reverse control* is brought into play. As soon as grasping contact has been made, the attacker reverses his muscular tension (Photo 42). Instead of trying to force the knife at the victim, the attacker starts pulling the knife away. This creates tension in the arm and body, but also it gives control of the knife to the victim. The victim now can do with the knife what he wishes; he may

49

pull it close to his chest or stomach. But under all circumstances, *the victim must be in total control of the knife.* This is the case regardless of whether the combatants are standing or are on the floor. If the kill is to occur in this locked combat, the victim carries off the mask and effects his own "killing."

If the encounter has the actors on the floor and a roll is to be staged, remember that the actors always roll away from the knife. If the knife is in the attacker's right hand, the roll would go to the attacker's left, keeping the knife away from the actors (Photo 43).

If the victim is to execute a throw on the attacker, it is best to have disarmament occur first. Depending on who is to end up with the blade, the disarmament must succeed in placing the knife where it can easily be picked up by the appropriate person. If the attacker must maintain control of the blade throughout the throw, the routine must be practiced many times in slow motion to make sure the knife is not going to come in contact with either of the combatants and that it will be held away from the attacker as he executes his fall. It is best to use a substitute prop—a soft rubber knife or one cut from light cardboard—rather than a real knife in the beginning practice sessions.

If you want to show the knife going into the victim, the only way to execute such a stunt safely is to have a knife with a retractable blade. One can be purchased in some gag shops and from theatre supply houses.

If you want a knife to be stuck into a character on stage and have it remain in the body, you would be wisest to abandon the idea—too many short cuts have ended in tragedy. Carried out in the professional theatre, this stunt requires a prosthetic device which conforms to the part of the body into which the knife is to be thrust. This device must have a backing through which a knife *cannot penetrate* as well as padding which will receive and retain the knife. Realism of this sort is not essential. Audiences come to the theatre willing to suspend a degree of disbelief. Remember that wood will split. This stunt is best avoided entirely.

Because audiences willingly suspend disbelief, their most important needs are to be able to empathize with characters, to get caught up in the excitement of a story line, and to enjoy the magic of illusion. Stage combat involving knives never should attempt a degree of realism that denies audiences the opportunity to exercise their vivid imaginations.

Photo 43a

Photo 43b

Photo 43c

50

NOTES

NOTES

Chapter 11
USING GUNS

Photo 44

A person once decided it would be great fun to put flash powder in an ashtray that was to be used as a prop in a stage production. You can see what the results may be—burned hands and possible blindness. The same mentality led another prankster to put a live round of ammo

Photo 45

in a gun that was to be used in a high school production; as a result, somebody got shot. Because *all guns are dangerous, they must be totally under the control of one responsible properties person.* Whenever guns are used on stage, *total awareness is a must.* The attacker should not place his finger on the trigger until he is to fire the gun. If for some reason the appearance of the finger's being on the trigger is thought necessary, then it should be pressed forward against the front of the trigger guard until the trigger is to be pulled (Photo 44). When the shot is fired at a distance of more than eight feet, it should be directed upstage of the victim by at least three feet (Photo 45). The illusion will work perfectly well if the gun is raised and fired quickly.

If you or an adult friend does not know guns and gun safety thoroughly, you should approach a police officer about coming to aid in the demonstration and practice of shooting scenes. The instructor, the director, or the officer should do several things to inform and give experience to the class:

1. Show a shotgun, a rifle, an automatic pistol, and a revolver to the class, explaining the mechanics of each.

2. Show how to check each kind of gun to determine whether it is loaded or has the potential of having a cartridge thrust into its firing chamber.

3. Demonstrate, with the handgun, at least three different loads of blanks and show what the blanks can do to six

or eight thicknesses of paper or a piece of cloth (e.g., powder burns, wad projectiles, and holes blown through material or into soft clay).

4. By shooting the gun several times, accustom students to the noise so they won't be so startled that they break character in a production.

5. Have students handle guns so as to reduce fear of the weapons.

6. Fire the gun *after* pointing it three feet upstage of each actor at a distance of twelve feet.

7. Urging extreme caution, have each student shoot the gun "at" other actors at the above-mentioned distances.

8. Teach students that pointing a gun is the same as pointing a finger; this encourages students to be accurate about where they point a gun.

Any handgun or rifle to be used on stage need not be larger than .22 caliber. Blanks with several strengths of load may be purchased at most lumber yards or sporting goods stores. Blank powder is black powder, and is highly corrosive on any weapon—most owners do not allow blanks to be shot in their guns. When shooting blanks, thorough cleaning after use is a must.

If a shot is to be fired point blank, then the gun must be covered and the shot directed to one side of the body —taking care not to allow the muzzle of the gun to make contact with skin or clothing (Photo 46). At close range, a blank can kill; even at long distances it can burn or blind an actor, depending on the size of the weapon and the blank. Never point the gun at head or face. Always direct the shot a short distance away from the lower midsection of your target. *Exercise extreme caution.*

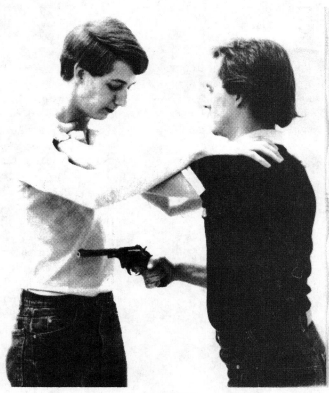

Photo 46

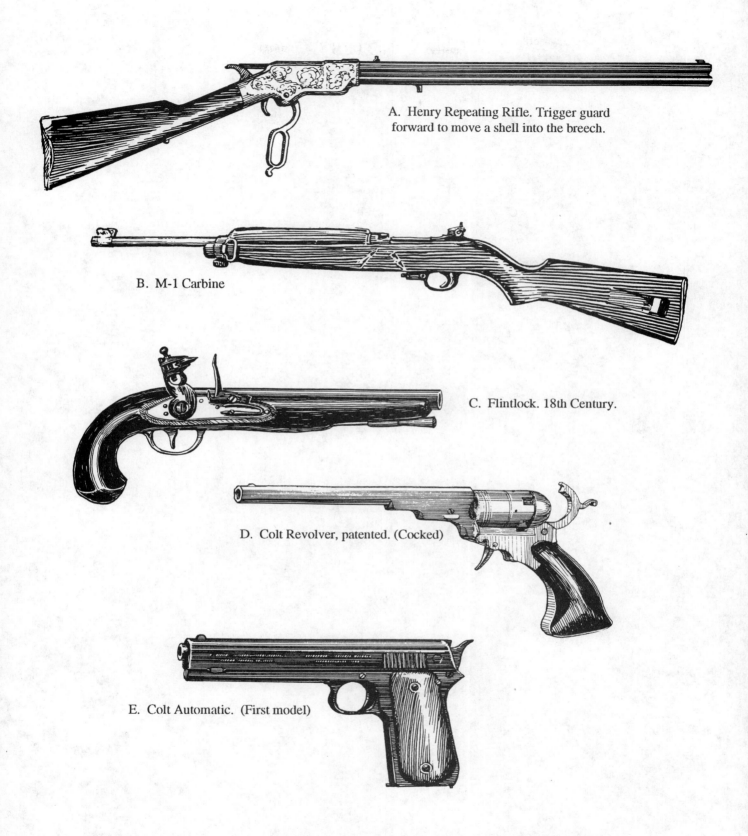

A. Henry Repeating Rifle. Trigger guard
forward to move a shell into the breech.

B. M-1 Carbine

C. Flintlock. 18th Century.

D. Colt Revolver, patented. (Cocked)

E. Colt Automatic. (First model)

Plate 11. Weapons. The important isuue is to understand the differences between hand guns and rifles as well as the
basic difference between automatic and action weapons. There are many variations of rifles and hand guns; the
above are just a small sampling.

NOTES

Chapter 12
STRIKING FROM BEHIND

Being hit from behind with any kind of instrument is dangerous, and on stage this kind of stunt requires perfect timing. No matter whether it's a club, gun, wrench, or whatever, contact is made; however, the contact that is made is only the forearm or hand to the back of the victim. The blow is softened at contact, and the victim is pushed. The implement is directed to one side of the back of the head, just a few inches away from the head (Photo 47). The attack is signaled by a stage sound (expulsion of air, click of the tongue, or light snap of fingers), masked upstage of the body, which begins the count. Both the attacker and the victim must practice the count so much together that the timing is perfect. The rhythm of the count, action, and reaction must work perfectly together for the action to be effective, as well as for the actors to be safe.

If you want actual contact in this kind of attack, then you must employ lightweight break-away devices. Break-away stools, boards, chairs, etc., can be made from balsa or styrofoam. Break-away bottles or mugs can be purchased from theatre specialty houses.

Balsa is expensive and time consuming and difficult to repair and reuse. Styrofoam must be covered lightly with papier-mache or muslin and then painted. When broken, it can be recovered, repainted, and reused.

Break-away bottles, glasses, windows, and the like are expensive. Made of sugar glass or resin, they also are very fragile. If you choose to use any of these items, remember that exerting too much pressure in holding them or too much force in swinging them may cause them to break before they actually make contact with the victim. Such items can be used only once; they cannot be repaired.

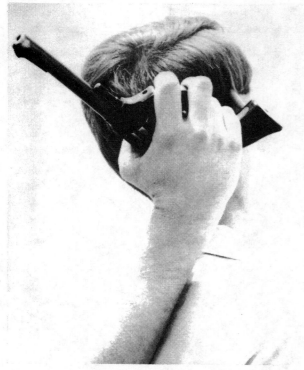

Photo 47a

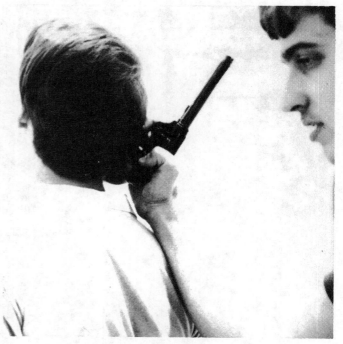

Photo 47b

NOTES

Chapter 13
USING WHIPS

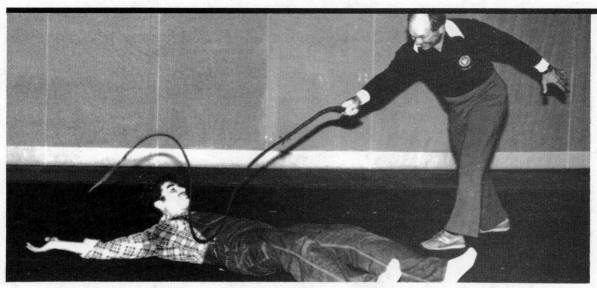

Photo 48a

The whip is a dangerous weapon under any circumstances, whether it's a toy or the real thing. First, the user must realize that what causes a whip to pop or snap is the fact that its tip is traveling faster than the speed of sound, which is roughly 1100 feet per second. In effect, the whip breaks the sound barrier, making a minisonic boom. Any object large enough to be visible which travels faster than the speed of sound is going to do damage if it comes in contact with the body. A whip can cut the skin or put out an aye, and it can injure the handler as well as his target. Therefore, the danger area encompasses a circle scribed by the length of the whip plus the length of the user's arm as its radius.

Use of the whip requires a great deal of practice, as well as total awareness of distance and surroundings. To prevent the whip from backlashing and thus injuring the user, he or she should relax the whip immediately following the check. The whip can be used to capture or encircle a receptor by softly lashing it around the waist, legs, or arms. The length of the whip and its distance from the receptor are vital to this stunt. Never should a whip be directed toward anyone's head or neck.

To practice with whips, go outdoors, where there is

plenty of room. Stage whips should be no longer than six to eight feet. Bull whips, not quirts, should be used. The former has a very short handle (eight or ten inches) and is made of braided leather, with a gradual taper leading to the end. Consequently, almost the entire length of the whip is flexible. The quirt, on the other hand, has a longer handle that is thin and flexible with a relatively short lash, braided on the end. This type of whip is not long enough to soften the blow, and it is rigid enough and small enough to hurt an actor upon contact.

The receptor should be lying on the floor. The attacker must know the distance of his reach and not stray from it while "whipping" the receptor. Contact is made with the middle third of the whip (Photo 48a), and the force must be relaxed just prior to that contact. When the stunt is performed correctly, the end of the whip (approximately two or three feet) slaps the floor on the far side of the receptor; the middle of the whip (the blow relaxed and pulled) lies fairly gently across the body (Photos 48b and 49); the receptor winces in pain; the attacker snarls in anger; and the audience cringes in fear. But no one has been hurt. If there are other actors on stage, they must be situated so as not to be within reach of the whip.

59

Photo 48b

Photo 49

60

NOTES

Plate 12. *Macbeth* — Southwestern Oklahoma State University.

Chapter 14
SWORD FIGHTING
FOIL, SABER, and LONG SWORD

Photo 50a

Photo 50b

In period plays sword-fighting scenes are fairly common. There are several good sources on period weapons and fencing practices in various historical periods, but period weapons and styles are not the subject of this chapter. Instead, let's look at the basics, the conditioning, and safety measures.

Fencing

At first, fencing maneuvers must be practiced with an imaginary opponent. Never begin with fencers facing each other.

Although stage fencing is very different from competition fencing, some of the same basics apply: proper conditioning; correct stance; conventional attack and retreat movements; and thrusts, parries, and ripostes. Let's begin with the *en garde* position for foil (Photo 50). The back foot (left foot for a right-handed fencer and vice versa) is turned at a ninety-degree angle to the front foot, which is pointing directly toward the direction of motion. From heel to heel, the feet should be apart about the distance of the width of the fencer's shoulders. The body should be in profile to the view of the opponent, with the face turned to look directly over the shoulder of the fencing arm. The elbow should be bent so that the upper arm is at approximately a 45-degree angle to the side of the body; the hand holds the foil as if it were an

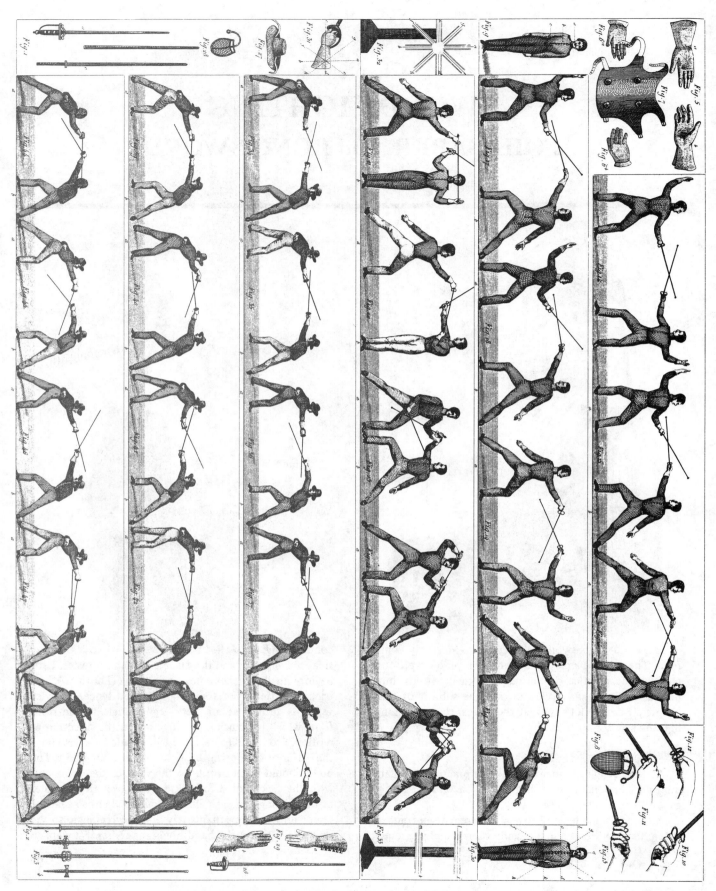

Plate 13. Military fencing from the ICONOGRAPHIC ENCYCLOPEDIA OF SCIENCE, LITERATURE AND ART by J.G. Heck.

Plate 14. Illustrations from Mr. Angel's THE SCHOOL OF FENCING WITH A GENERAL EXPLANATION OF THE PRINCIPAL ATTITUDES AND POSITIONS PECULIAR TO THE ART (1787). Here we see "The guard of the sword and lantern opposed by the sword and cloak," (Top) and "The defensive guard of the small-sword against the broad sword" (Bottom).

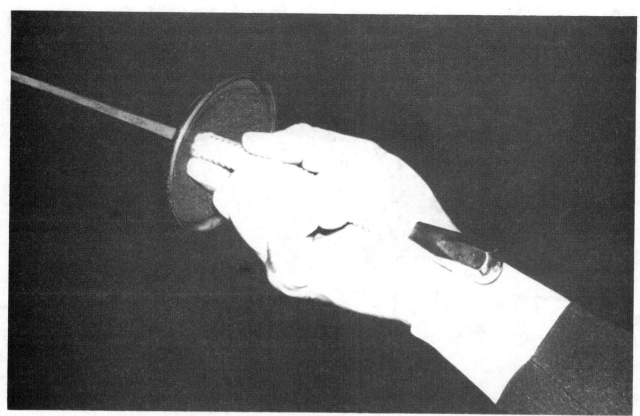

Photo 51

extension of the forearm. The tip of the foil (a small three-foot dowel can be used when foils are unavailable) should be pointed at the eyes of the opponent. The hand should grasp the handle of the foil with the forefinger curled and pressed against the bell-guard (under the handle), the remaining three fingers grasping the handle, and the thumb on top of the handle and in line with the handle (Photo 51). The rear arm is extended out and flexed so that the hand is held approximately head high.

Using the proper grip and assuming the correct stance, actors now may begin to practice attack and retreat movements. The attack involves stepping forward with the front foot, keeping the toe pointed toward the opponent. As the heel of the front foot makes contact with the floor, the rear foot is brought forward to assume the same position as the *en garde*. This process is repeated to carry the fencer forward. To retreat, the process is reversed: the rear foot moves first, and the front foot is brought back to the *en garde* position. These movements must be practiced repeatedly to get muscles in shape. The unusual positions bring into use muscles that seldom are exercised, and soreness is likely after the first two or three days of practice.

The next moves to be mastered are the thrust and lunge. The sword-fighter's purpose here is to run the blade through an opponent. The thrust is simply moving the foil forward to its furthest extension by straightening the arm in the direction of the opponent. The lunge is carried out by keeping the rear foot in place and stepping forward with the front foot to its greatest extension while leaving room for the knee to flex or land just over the toe of the front foot (Photo 52). The rear arm and hand drop to a parallel position on the lunge and then return to the *en garde* stance when the lunge is recovered. This exercise must be repeated many times in order to develop balance and strength in its execution.

Now is a good time to put it all together. Have the fencers, at your command, attack—retreat—attack—lunge and thrust—retreat—attack, and so forth.

The Saber

After working with foils for two or three days, you may want to progress to the saber. The *en garde* stance (feet and body) is the same for this weapon. The differences are that the rear hand is not held high but is instead placed on the rear hip or side. Sometimes it may be held in the small of the back, but this is mainly for show and is a dangerous maneuver. The grip on the saber should be the same except that the tip is not pointed at the eyes of the opponent. The saber is held tip up, but at a 45-degree angle across the fencer's body (Photo 53) with the extension of the bell-guard protecting the hand from the opponent's attack (Photo 54). The saber's tip can inflict damage, but the saber primarily is a slashing (swashbuckling) sword. The attack, retreat, and lunge are the same as those involving the foil, although the thrust in this case is a slashing rather than a stabbing motion. Remember to keep the rear hand on the hip or side at all times. The openness, the flair, the showmanship can all come later, after the discipline has been mastered.

Photo 52

Photo 53

Photo 54

Attacks and Parries

Now is the time to learn the different attacks and the appropriate parries (blocks) for each. Actors should begin working in pairs. In foil there are two primary parries —to the right and to the left. If the attack is coming on the inside (front part of the body) of the defender, the parry is to the left (if the defender is right handed). The parry is accomplished by keeping the elbow stationary, catching the opponent's blade on the shank (the heavy part), and moving the wrist slightly to the left, causing the tip of the opponent's blade to pass by the body of the defender (Photo 55). The parry to the right is accomplished by moving the wrist to the right, again causing the tip of the opponent's blade to pass by the back of the defender (Photo 56). In both cases, as the hand/wrist moves to the left/right, the elbow remains stationary; the tip of the blade of the defender also should remain in the same relative position as it is when *en garde*. Following a parry, the defender should return to a neutral or *en garde* position, unless he or she takes advantage of the successful parry by riposting (going on the attack) and thus becoming the aggressor. Practice parries to the left and right at half speed, working up to full speed.

In saber, there are five practical parries: head (Photo 57), high inside (Photo 58), high outside (Photo 59), low inside (Photo 60), and low outside (Photo 61). The parry for the head attack is to raise the saber parallel to the floor, high enough to catch the opponent's blade and to keep it from making contact with the defender's head. The parry for the high inside attack is made with the tip of the blade up and the blade perpendicular to the floor, warding off the attack that is coming at the upper half of the torso to the front side of the body. For both the upper inside and upper outside parries, the defender's blade is moved out to make contact with the opposing blade prior to its reaching the defender's body. The low inside and low outside parries are made with the tip of the blade pointing down to the floor but with the same action as above to keep the opponent's blade from making contact with the defender. Practice these parries repeatedly at half speed, later increasing to full speed.

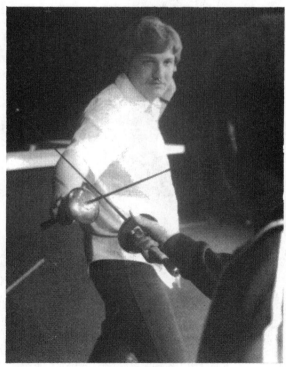

Photo 56

68

Photo 58

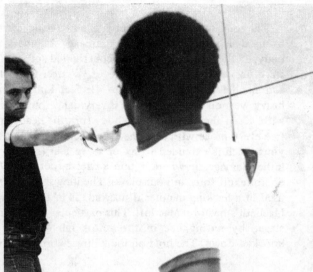

Photo 59

Photo 60

Photo 61

Fencing Terminology

Following is an explanation of some basic terms in fencing.

Beat: A beat is simply the striking together of blades. The beat is used to set up the attack (e.g., beat-thrust, beat-thrust, beat-thrust, beat-disengage-thrust and lunge). In effect the fencer sets a rhythm and then breaks it in order to try to catch the opponent off guard. Beats are done to the right and/or left sides of the blade.

Disengage: To disengage means simply to move the blade to the opposite side of the opponent's blade. The aim is to change the line of attack from inside (the front part of the opponent's body) to outside (the back side of the opponent's body). This is carried out with a slight wrist action, dropping the tip of the blade underneath the blade of the opponent. A single disengage moves the blade to the opposite side from which the fencer began. A double disengage goes to the opposite side and then returns to the original one. If a fencer is quick enough, he or she may effect a triple disengage: three crosses under the opponent's blade prior to a thrust and lunge.

Cutover: The cutover is a move which, like the disengage, serves to change the line of attack, except that in this case the tip of the blade is raised and passes over the top of the opponent's blade.

Envelopment: This move is an attempt to disarm the opponent. The opponent's blade is controlled by the shank (heavy part) of the attacker's blade, the tip of which encircles the opponent's blade two or three times with a wrist check on the upper or lower half of the encirclement. This sharp check of the wrist may pull the blade out of the opponent's hand. Envelopment usually is done counterclockwise against a right-handed fencer and clockwise against a left-handed one because it is easier to break a grip away from the thumb than from the fingers.

Feint: A feint is a move in a direction which the fencer does not really intend to take. The aim is to draw the opponent out of line or off balance.

Sword and Dagger

Sometimes a combat scene may involve the use of both sword and dagger by each actor, thus involving both hands with dangerous weapons (Photo 62). If the weapons are to be kept in control of the actors, the combat should be restricted to attack/parry up until the final thrust. If, however, safe disarmaments can be effected, more activity may ensue once the combatants are restricted to a single weapon each. Judge the danger in such scenes, acting according to good sense.

Long Sword

The long sword (battle sword) is a two-handed weapon used in slashing attacks to the head, shoulders, and body. If these swords are to be constructed specially for stage use, they should be made of ¼" steel with blade and handle approximately 4 to 4½ feet long. Being a heavy weapon, the long sword is very dangerous to work with. Keep the attacks to the body (not the head); practice every move with extreme care, keeping in mind that your reach is extended to six or seven feet (so you can inflict damage anywhere within a twelve-foot diameter), do not exert force in your blows. The long sword may be used in a hacking manner if masked, as in the taking of Macbeth's head by Macduff. This particular scene can be staged by having one of the actors fall down or get knocked down. The hold on the killing sword is reversed

Photo 62

70

and used to "stab" the victim in a masked final blow (Photos 63, 64, and 65); then with a hacking attack (masked), striking a heavy sack of rags, the action is completed with the sound of the sword striking something soft. Place the artificial "head" on the end of the sword and raise it for the audience to see.

Photo 63

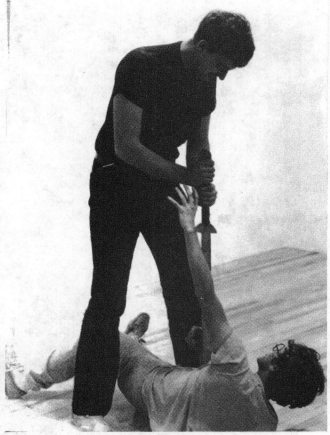

Photo 64

Photo 65

Choreographing the Sword Fight

When the appropriate skills detailed above have been mastered, a sword-fighting scene can be directed, and the audience will be excited and pleased. Remember, however, the primary purpose always is to maintain safety.

We do not strike at the head, or at least when we do, it is never with great force, unless a ducked blow is intended to produce a whistling blade; in such cases, the timing must be perfect. In fact, all sword-fighting scenes must be carefully choreographed with everything working according to plan. Much of the excitement and flair of a sword fight is an attack which the receiver must either duck or jump over. Knowing when to duck or jump is important because a blade traveling fast enough to "swoosh" through the air (a sound audiences love), is traveling fast enough to do a lot of damage to anything it might strike.

The proper moves are set up by telegraphing the attack and looking at the target (Photo 66). When we add the telegraph and the look to an already planned sequence, real communication takes place between the fencers, and the stunt works well. In the case of both the duck and the jump, the action of the receiver precedes the attack.

Following is one such sequence:

Beat

Beat-Disengage-Thrust

Beat Attacker draws back arm and sword for head attack and looks at head (the telegraphed move).

Receiver ducks.

Attacker swings with force in move designed to decapitate opponent.

Opponent regains stance and fight resumes.

Beat

Beat-X (receiver becomes attacker)

Beat-Cutover-Thrust and Lunge

Recover

Beat Attacker draws back arm and sword and looks at opponent's feet (the telegraphed move).

Receiver jumps.

Attacker swings under feet.

Recover and continue.

With this kind of communication through the sword fight, which has been carefully planned, the combatants are aware constantly of each other's intent, allowing the fight to be conducted with excitement and safety.

Photo 66a

Following are some symbols that should help you as you choreograph sword-fighting scenes. Instructions are given from the point of view of the attacker. Remember that the defender always is parrying and trying to avoid being touched or "killed."

BR—Beat right, strike blade from right side
BL—Beat left, strike blade from left side
D—Single disengage
D2—Double disengage
D3—Triple disengage
T—Thrust
L—Lunge
TL—Thrust and lunge
CO—Cutover
En—Envelopment
FR—Feint right
FL—Feint left
Dis—Disarm
Ex—Exchange, defender becomes attacker
SH—Singing blade at head
SF—Singing blade at feet
XRL—Defender and attacker exchange positions Left and Right
—*—Wound
—†—Kill

For most acting needs there are three styles of sword fighting: Shakespearean, which is stalking and crude; swashbuckling (sabers), which features an open stance with broad action and much flair; and late French (17th-18th century), which is characterized by finesse.

A kill is performed on stage by having the blade pass "through" on the upstage side of the body. This action is best done quickly, and it must be masked. The most effective way to carry out this maneuver is to thrust the tip of the blade between the victim's upstage side and arm (the tip just past the body and clear of any entanglement in the costume) and to lunge quickly. The blade should be withdrawn quickly as the fencers separate and the death scene begins.

The actor who is to die needs to understand that there are two important factors to consider. First, he must convey a look of stunned shock; second, he must carry off a response which is much like having the wind knocked out of him.

Remember that regardless of whether you are using the real thing or any of various substitutes, you are dealing with an extremely dangerous weapon. If not used properly, such instruments can put out eyes and even kill. Show respect and concern for yourself and others by always being *en garde.*

Photo 66b

Photo 66c

Plate 15. Rehearsal for the Players U.S.A./William Alan-Landes WONDRAWHOPPER, "Robin Hood," with steel bars, later to be finished as broad swords. (Left to Right) Prince John (Walter Scholz) Much the Miller's Son (Don Agey), testing their metal.

NOTES

Plate 16. *Guys and Dolls* — Southwestern Oklahoma State University.

Chapter 15
CHOREOGRAPHED FIGHTS
and GANG FIGHTS

Begin planning a choreographed fight by deciding which weapons you want to use. Begin with sequences involving pairs of actors, establishing a motivation for the fight (setting the scene). Work out each detail of the encounter, and do all the action in slow motion. Don't forget to include vocal details. Such an encounter should last no longer than 30-45 seconds and should involve no more than four or five different exercises.

Following is an example of such a sequence:

Man and woman (A & B) are walking through the park. Man (C) accosts woman (B). Man A then pushes C down and starts to take woman away. C grabs A by one arm and throws him across the stage. A does a lateral roll, gets up, and squares off with C. C throws a roundhouse punch at A, who breaks the punch and does a shoulder throw which sends C into a back shoulder roll. Woman kicks C in the stomach and screams for police. C gets up and starts to run off, holding stomach, while A boots C in the rear as they exit stage.

A second example:

Woman A is walking through the park. Man B, drunk, accosts her. Being a karate expert, she steps to her right with her right foot and delivers a left-foot kick to his mid-section. As B bends over, A delivers a karate chop to the back of his neck. A finally gives him a kick to the mid-section, and he rolls off the front of the stage.

Exercise your own imagination and choreograph other encounters involving a pair of actors, repeating them numerous times to give actors experience. You are then ready to proceed to fight sequences involving three persons.

Following is an example of a three-person sequence:

Older man or woman A is accosted by two young punks B and C. B pushes A backward and begins to do it again, when A grabs one arm and gives B a shoulder throw. C approaches A from behind, but A turns and kicks C in the side, causing him to fall down. B, having regained his feet, grabs A from behind in an arm-pinning bear hug. A stomps B's instep, breaking the hold. B grabs foot, and A does a knee-lift, which knocks B out as he falls off the stage, but as A bends over to pick a flower, C falls over him/her to the lip of the stage before falling off. A leaves smelling the flower.

Have the class choreograph several trio combat numbers.

The last kind of exercise in group combat is the gang fight. This can be set up as a planned "rumble" or as a "domino-effect" involvement. The most important thing to remember in planning a gang fight is that each set of fighters must remain in their appointed areas most of the time. If, for example, you have twelve people fighting, you could have two actors downstage right, three center stage, three upstage left, four upstage right. A fight of this size should move. In the example cited, you would have three areas where members from one group could move to another: one from the group up right could be pushed into the center-stage group; then that new person and one of the actors originally center stage could have a fight down left, and so forth. Naturally, an encounter of this sort must be exceptionally well timed and rehearsed.

The fight scene must have more rehearsal than any other scene in a show. It must be rehearsed until the timing is exactly right and always the same. One slight change in timing or slight loss of concentration can lead to serious injury.

A stage combat show is a fitting conclusion to a course in stage combat, and it even can be used as part of a final test. Your audience will find it both enlightening and entertaining. Such a show should feature each of the learned maneuvers and stunts.

Always work for professionalism in your presentation of stage combat.

Break a leg . . . but do it safely.

NOTES

INDEX

CLAUDE D. KEZER teaches a course in Stage Combat and Safety at Southwestern Oklahoma State University. The course design is based on Professor Kezer's personal experience as an actor and an athlete. "My experience in stage combat techniques comes from doing, observing, and thinking through routines and exercises," he says. As a football player, a member of the University of Oklahoma fencing team, and a staff sergeant in the U. S. Air Force, he learned to protect himself in dangerous situations. During his 31 years in professional theatre as an actor, singer, dancer, and director, he used his athletic and military training to embellish his skills in stage combat. He has directed approximately 45 plays and musicals.

His education includes the Bachelor of Fine Arts and Master of Fine Arts degrees from the University of Oklahoma. His stage-related memberships include Actors Equity Association, American Theatre Association, Southwest Theatre Conference, Oklahoma Theatre Center, Oklahoma Theatre Education Association, and Weatherford Fine Arts Council.